Original title:
Verses from the Void

Copyright © 2025 Creative Arts Management OÜ
All rights reserved.

Author: Amelia Montgomery
ISBN HARDBACK: 978-1-80567-764-2
ISBN PAPERBACK: 978-1-80567-885-4

Chronicles of Ethereal Shadows

In the gloom where shadows play,
A ghost tried to sing, but lost his way.
He tripped on a thought, fell into a rhyme,
Now he dances with echoes, wasting time.

A cloud in a hurry, forgot its rain,
It laughed at the sun, called it mundane.
While planets giggled, twirled in delight,
A star winked, saying, 'Isn't this light?'

Insights from the Celestial Veil

A comet sneezed, oh what a sight!
Spreading stardust all through the night.
The moon rolled her eyes, said, 'Not again!'
While the earth donned a jacket from the rain.

Whispers of asteroids filled the air,
'Who let the meteors eat our hair?'
Galaxies laughed, in a cosmic jest,
'They're just space rocks, we know best.'

Dimensions Beyond the Grasp

In a realm where socks vanish and hide,
Dimensions of laundry we cannot abide.
One sock may dwell in a cosmic place,
A black hole of threads, lost in the space.

There are timelines where cats run the show,
With rulers and crowns, they prowl to and fro.
While dogs chase tails, pondering the stars,
In their own silly world of barking guitars.

Thoughts in the Twilight

As twilight breaks, ideas begin to sprout,
A thought bubble pops, while owls shout.
The trees gossip softly, sharing a laugh,
A firefly's dance, the light's epitaph.

A moth in a tux tried to crash the ball,
But the flame's a diva, and gave it a call.
With a wink and a twirl, it spun to the tune,
Dancing with shadows under the moon.

Shadows Cast by Starlight

In the dark, a cat wore shades,
Swinging its tail, all in parades.
Whispers of giggles float in the air,
As stars play hide-and-seek without a care.

A moonbeam slipped, fell on the street,
Laughed with a potato, now that's a treat!
Dancing shadows prance like folks in disguise,
Keeping time with the winks from the skies.

A comet with tea, pouring for the night,
Told tales of dust bunnies taking flight.
Twinkling laughter, a cosmic delight,
As planets hoot jokes, making trouble in sight.

Galactic giggles, the universe sings,
Woolly worm travelers on bicycle swings.
Each twinkle a wink, the cosmos conspires,
In this silly dance, our whimsy never tires.

Sentences in the Ethereal Light

Floating words in the beams aglow,
Scribbling stories the shadows don't know.
A pun in the language of glowing dust,
Makes even the starlings break out in rust.

Chasing after whispers with glee and delight,
A unified giggle in the soft velvet night.
Puns offered freely by squirrels in flight,
Twirling around moons that shine oh so bright.

Gravity giggles, even stars lose their way,
Bouncing on orbits like children at play.
They trade cosmic quirks, a celestial show,
As glittering winks in the dark overflow.

So let's toast to the laughter that twinkles and glows,
Where cosmic kittens break all of the prose.
In these playful moments, let joy take its flight,
As sentences dance in the ethereal light.

Whispers of the Abyss

In the deep, a fish asked,
"Hey, do you know my name?"
The depths just shrugged back,
"I forgot, it's all the same!"

A jellyfish dancing bright,
Wobbly in watery light,
Said, "Why don't we have teeth?"
"Because we snack on delight!"

A crab clacked a joke near,
"Life's a pinch, don't you see?"
With claws held high in cheer,
"If it pinches, it's still free!"

The octopus waved in glee,
"Eight arms mean more to eat!"
"And if I feel lonely,"
"I can hug my own feet!".

Echoes in the Silence

Quiet echoes start to tease,
Bouncing off the walls with ease.
A whisper said, "I just got lost!"
"Take a map, but at what cost?"

With a giggle in the air,
The silence danced without a care.
"Did you hear that? Oh, what a tune!"
"Just crickets playing under the moon!"

Muffled laughter fills the void,
As a sock puppet gets employed.
"I'm not just fabric, I've got flair!"
"Well, brush your teeth—don't forget hair!"

Inside the stillness, jokes abound,
In moments where no sounds are found.
A tinkle here, a chuckle there,
Echoes weaving through open air!.

Shadows of the Unseen

In the dark, shadows do prance,
Tiptoeing like they're in a dance.
"How do we keep out of sight?"
"By moving left, then, oh what a fright!"

A shadow sneezed and ran away,
"Excuse me, I'm allergic to gray!"
The light said, "Stay away from me!"
"Or I might just turn you into tea!"

A grayscale party kicked off strong,
With phantom tunes and ghostly song.
"Come join us, don't be a bore!"
"Just step in, and we'll ask for more!"

The unseen made quite the mess,
With laughter echoes and no distress.
As shadows stacked upon the floor,
They laughed and pranced forevermore!.

Lullabies of the Infinite

In a dream where giggles roam,
A cat serenades a gnome.
"Hush now, it's time to drift away,"
"But just one more joke, then I'll stay!"

Count the stars in funny hats,
Each one giggles with the bats.
"Is that a comet, or just my mom?"
"If it's her, you better stay calm!"

Twirling planets hum along,
To the lull of cosmic song.
"Wrap me up, I'm getting cold!"
"But can I wear your space-age gold?"

As dreams unfold in joyful light,
The universe whispers to the night.
"Here's a giggle, float away,
With lullabies that always play!.

Lullabies of the Eternal Silence

In a world where shadows play,
The crickets hum the night away.
A ghostly cat chases its tail,
Whiskers twitching without fail.

The moon yawns wide, a sleepy ball,
Waves of silence start to crawl.
A star winks down with a grin,
As if the fun is about to begin.

In the stillness, a snore resounds,
Echoes bounce in circular bounds.
Sleepy time for the wandering ghost,
While other spirits just want to boast.

So as you close your weary eyes,
Remember the antics in the skies.
For in deep slumber, laughter lies,
And whispers gather in gentle sighs.

Fragments from the Abyss

Beneath the waves, the fish all rant,
A sea sponge plays the bouzouki chant.
Octopus juggling laughter's tease,
While seahorses giggle with ease.

A jellyfish does a playful jig,
Bobbing along, feeling quite big.
The crabs join in, doing the twist,
In the tide's embrace, they cannot resist.

In the tight-knit crew of the deep blue,
Each creature's weird, but so much fun too.
From starfish bops to the clownfish jest,
The depths can be silly, just like the rest.

So, come take a dive where giggles swell,
In this water party, all is well.
With laughter echoing through the abyss,
It's a comedic world, can't you see this?

Voices from the Dark

In the midnight hush, owls hoot jokes,
While shadows play at playing folk.
The moles organize a surprise show,
Underneath the ground, where no one will go.

The bats swoop low, wearing capes of grace,
Dancing around in a wild embrace.
Their echoing giggles fill the air,
As they swing and sway without a care.

A ghost appears—his dance is a fright,
But his moves are funny in the pale moonlight.
With a cackle and howl, he flees with a shout,
Chasing squirrels who tumble about.

Laughter sprouts in the darkest place,
Where fears dissolve into merry grace.
In this nocturnal comedy brigade,
Even the night fears do not invade.

Sonnets of the Shadows

Shadows gather, plotting their schemes,
Scheming to give us funny dreams.
A waltz with the wispy and spry,
As they tickle the night, oh my!

The specters conspire for a grand parade,
Creating mischief in their charade.
With each glimmer, a giggle goes round,
As the spookier bits of life abound.

They frolic and dance, how they delight,
In shadows that spill into the light.
With a wink and a nudge, they take a bow,
Oh, the joys of the spectral wow!

So if you trip through the twilight's grace,
Find the laughter hidden in the space.
For in shadows where chuckles bloom,
There's a comedy waiting in every room.

Reflections in the Depths

In a place where shadows bounce,
The cat debates its sense of pounce,
A fish in space, a cosmic cat,
Chasing dreams, or was it that?

On a chair made out of air,
A ghost pretends it's got a care,
It sips its tea from cups of night,
And giggles at the moon's delight.

A sock escapes from laundry hell,
Into the void, it starts to dwell,
Finding freedom, not alone,
It waltzes with a talking stone.

A jester sings of folly's cheer,
In the dark, we smell the fear,
Yet laughter echoes through the stars,
Socks and stones, the cosmic bazars.

Poems Written in Starlight

A comet hiccups in its flight,
A turtle glows with all its might,
It pens a sonnet, not too bright,
Of cheese and grapes on a moonlit night.

The owl gives sage advice, then snores,
While meteors shine and play with roars,
A dragon's tail, it swishes wide,
In this ballet, there's no need to hide.

Stars are whispers, beams of jest,
In velvet skies, we do our best,
To write of things both bright and quirky,
Like space snacks that taste just like jerky.

A screen of dark, with laugh lines traced,
Where time and space both interlaced,
In starlit poems, chaos reigns,
Yet madness holds in joyful chains.

Notes from Beyond the Veil

A grapefruit floats, it had it tough,
In realms where ghosts just poke and bluff,
With wings made of paper, here they glide,
In this carnival, all spirits slide.

A distant tune of laughter rings,
As jellybeans sprout little wings,
They hum a song of cosmic cheer,
In this strange land, we shed our fear.

With cookies made of lunar dust,
We feast on dreams, it's quite a must,
A phantom chef in chef's attire,
Whips up a dish that's made of fire.

So take a bow, and share a glance,
In this strange world, we twirl and dance,
For notes from realms where shadows dwell,
Proclaim that life's a funny spell.

Ciphers of the Ethereal

A pencil sharpens in the void,
Where laughter echoes, never coyed,
A fish departs on laughing fits,
While birds recite their secret scripts.

In a garden made of jelly beans,
Dancing with sighs and silly scenes,
The roses hum a tune so sweet,
As fairies tap their tiny feet.

On stardust paths, we stroll and play,
With marshmallow moons that sway all day,
A riddle spun with threads of fun,
In the twilight where we all run.

These ciphers lead us round and round,
In cosmic circles, laughs abound,
For in each twist, a giggle lies,
In this ethereal game, we rise.

Songs of Lost Connections

My phone died mid-message, a real shock,
I typed a great tale, but it ended with 'Bok.'
The cat stared at me, as if to agree,
Life's one big joke, oh woe is me!

I tried to call you on my ancient phone,
But it rang like a fridge, all groans and moans.
You answered with laughter, but I couldn't hear,
So I texted a meme - you're my pal, my dear!

The Wi-Fi is down, what a tragic fate,
It left me with only my thoughts, oh mate.
I wrote a haiku about my lost friend,
But sent it to Grandma, she's not one to trend.

So here's to the times when connections run dry,
We laugh and we stumble, we reach for the sky.
In a world of dead signals, let humor abide,
For the punchlines delivered, we'll take in our stride.

Fragments from the Whispers

I heard a strange voice, oh what did it say?
Was it my coffee, or just yesterday?
It whispered, 'Get up!' but I wished it would quit,
The couch is too comfy, my heart won't permit.

A ghost in the hallway, or just my old broom?
It spun tales of past, while I surveyed my room.
Drinking cold leftovers, a meal from the fridge,
Funny how hunger makes me feel like a smidge.

There are echoes of laughter in the back of my mind,
A tune for the ages, a little unkind.
When the pie in my face felt like a big win,
Life's greatest lessons are soaked in some sin.

Here's to the moments where oddity reigns,
Where whispers of nonsense spark joy in our veins.
We dance with the echoes, we tango with glee,
In fragments of whispers, we just want to be!

Phrases Carved in Starlight

I caught a glimpse of a star that, alas,
Seemed to wink at me, with a giggle and sass.
It said, 'Write me a line, make it snappy and bright,'
But I tripped on a comet - oh what a sight!

Moonbeams were dancing, quite awkwardly so,
They slipped on their capes, gave a grand show.
My pen ran away, chased by hungry space rats,
Left me with craters and wandering chats.

Galaxies whispered, 'Your dreams are too big,'
I laughed at their fears, and did a small jig.
Each phrase carved in starlight, a cosmic jest,
I'll send it by rocket - it's bound to digress!

In the realm of the cosmos, we stumble and bounce,
Words floating like meteors, watch as they pounce.
A symphony crafted from twinkling delight,
Carving our laughter in the fabric of night.

Reverbs of the Dark Abyss

From depths of the dark, a sound starts to rise,
With echoes of whoopee cushions and sighs.
It tickles the void with absurdity's flair,
Where laughter grows wild, in the deep of despair.

The shadows are dancing, a lively parade,
With jokes made of stardust, in chorus displayed.
A punchline's emerging from caverns of low,
I'm stuck in a punchline, what a crazy show!

Spooky old specters, they whisper my name,
But I'm busy dodging their fruitcake of shame.
They serve up their humor, a banquet for me,
With rotten old jokes and a side of cold tea.

Reverbs of chaos, a raucous delight,
As the void spins around in a whirl of the night.
We're lost in the giggles, tangled in jest,
For laughter's the compass, we're finally blessed!

Starlit Dreams in the Gloom

In shadows where the giggles hide,
The moonlight dances, oh what a ride!
Starfish wear hats, the comets get bold,
While space squirrels tell tales from the old.

In dreams we chase a flying fish,
Wishing for a cosmic dish!
The planets laugh, they spin and twirl,
As gravity takes a silly whirl.

With each twinkle, a chuckle we find,
As the universe plays tricks, oh so kind!
Galaxies wink like cheeky sprites,
In the dark, laughter ignites.

So join the jesters of the night,
Where stardust giggles take flight.
In this place where fun unfolds,
The stories of space turn to gold.

Harmonies of the Hidden

Beneath the stars, a garden grows,
With flowers that tickle the toes!
The daisies hum a merry tune,
While the daisies send whispers to the moon.

The nightingale wears glasses so fine,
While crickets tap dance, keeping time.
Fireflies glow with a jovial zest,
Creating melodies, they do their best.

In this jungle of giggles, don't you see?
The owls are experts in comedy!
They hoot about socks that wander wide,
And shoes that dance with cosmic pride.

As laughter echoes through the trees,
The universe sways in the breeze.
So, grab a friend, and join the cheer,
In the hidden harmonies, we'll steer!

Rhythms Beyond the Horizon

Beyond the waves where jellybeans sway,
The sun wears pajamas, ready to play.
Bouncing clouds in a cheeky race,
While rainbows do cartwheels, oh what a place!

The tides are grinning, they splash with flair,
As sea turtles sing tunes of despair.
But fear not, for the humor's alive,
In the ocean where giggles thrive.

Driftwood creates a rhythm divine,
With shells that clink in a joyful line.
Dolphins tell jokes in flips and spins,
While the starfish chuckle at all the wins.

So sail on waves of giggling foam,
In this rhythm where laughter roams.
The horizon calls with a goofy grin,
Join the party, let the fun begin!

Secrets of the Starlit Silence

In the hush where giggles reside,
Secrets of laughter carefully hide.
Stars whisper jokes in cosmic bars,
While meteors hop like runaway cars.

The quiet winks with a chuckling sigh,
As galaxies waddle, oh my, oh my!
With suns that peek 'round stardust bends,
And wink at us like old friends.

Comets burst forth in dazzling lights,
Sharing stories of goofy sights.
From black holes pulling pranks so bold,
To cosmic clowns that never grow old.

So ride the quiet, the giggles unseal,
In the starlit silence, we truly feel.
For in each twinkle, a secret resides,
Of laughter and joy, where wonder abides.

Riddles of the Cosmic Silence

In endless dark, where whispers play,
A sock was lost, it stole away.
The stars complain of laundry woes,
While moons just giggle, strike a pose.

Black holes dance with gravity's flair,
Yet planets sigh, 'It's just not fair.'
Comets pass with a cheeky wink,
As asteroids debate, 'Do we stink?'

Refrains from the Forgotten Spaces

In an attic of dust, with dreams in stacks,
Old aliens plot, with jittery backs.
They ponder life, with cookie crumbs,
While time-travelers hum silly drums.

Glowing orbs start a karaoke night,
To sing about space and dream of flight.
But when they try to belt out tunes,
The vacuum laughs, shaking its moons.

Dreams Scattered Among the Stars

A galaxy's quilt with patches bright,
Containing jokes from asteroids in flight.
They chuckle at comets, who zoom and dash,
While meteors argue, 'I'm not so brash!'

Dreams drift along with a humorous flair,
While space whales giggle, giving despair.
They swim through the night, with bubbles of glee,
Telling tales of the stars, so wild and free.

Monologues of the Uncharted

A black cat crossed a starry road,
The cosmos paused, its fate bestowed.
It stumbled near a cosmic pie,
And baked a cake that made suns cry.

Planets gather for a sitcom night,
Spilling coffee and cracking light.
They brainstorm plots of far-off lands,
While meteor showers wave their hands.

Fables from the Starlit Deep

In the dark, a fish wore shoes,
Dancing all night, with nothing to lose.
He bumped a star, said, "What a thrill!"
"Careful there, buddy, you're giving me chills!"

A crab found a hat, quite a delight,
Proclaimed himself king, but was far from bright.
He tried to decree with a shell on his ear,
But the other sea critters just laughed, "Oh dear!"

A jellyfish laughed, pulsing with pride,
"At the disco, I've got nothing to hide!"
But he floated too high, missed the dance floor,
"Next time," he said, "I'll bring my own door."

So gather around, in this strange tidal wave,
Where laughter and music forever behave.
In depths of the dark, where the silly reside,
Even the void has a giggling side!

Chronicles of the Cosmic Whisper

A comet passed by with a wink and a grin,
Laughed at the planets, said, "Where to begin?"
"Your orbits are strange, but that's not a crime,"
"I'll race you to Mars, we'll make it in time!"

The sun turned around, wearing shades of gold,
"Is this a race, or are we just bold?"
The stars crowded close, cheering loud like a cheer,
"Light up the path, the finish line's near!"

Through nebula clouds, they stumbled and spun,
With laughter like echoes, they raced just for fun.
Until they all found, to their sheer delight,
That laughing together felt just so right.

So next time you gaze at the night up above,
Remember the whispers, the laughter, the love.
For in every orbit, in each twinkling eye,
Are tales of the cosmos, just waiting to fly!

Echoes in the Abyss

In the abyss, a cat wore a hat,
Said to the squid, "I'm the next cool cat!"
The squid blinked twice, gave a curl of a tentacle,
"But cats can't swim; you're just being cynical!"

A dolphin swam by with a bubble of cheer,
"Let's tell some jokes, they won't bite or smear!"
But the sharks just yawned, far too busy to laugh,
"We're planning our lunch, can you hurry up, chaff?"

Then came a whale, booming tales of old,
"Who told the deep secrets, who's ever so bold?"
With a splash and a dance, they all gathered near,
In the echoes of laughter, their worries disappeared.

So if you take a plunge and dive down to play,
Remember that laughter can brighten your day.
In shadows so deep, find the funny that flies,
And let the abyss fill with hilarious cries!

Whispers of the Eternal Night

In the eternal night, a mouse with a dream,
Thought he could fly with a paper ice cream.
He stumbled and tumbled, then cried with delight,
"Next time I'll soar, just hang on tight!"

A bat, swooping low, found the misfit so dear,
"Join me in the sky, it's safer up here!"
But the mouse shook his head, with a giggle and grin,
"With wings made of paper, there's no way I'll win!"

The stars twinkled back, giggling so bright,
As the mouse dreamed of sailing way up in the night.
In shadows, they danced to a whimsical tune,
With the moon nodding slow, like a giant balloon.

So in every giggle, in every mishap,
There's magic afoot, in the nighttime trap.
For laughter's the secret of this cosmic play,
Where dreams take flight, and the night rules the day!

Musical Echoes from the Void

In a land where socks all dance,
A tune is played by ants in pants.
The moonlight winks with giggles bright,
As shadows tickle, taking flight.

A cowbell rings, a rubber band,
The llamas join a marching band.
They sing of pies and silly songs,
While chairs wear hats and dance along.

The echoes tickle, twist and sway,
As ducks on skateboards glide and play.
The stars all laugh, the planets grin,
In this grand ball where jokes begin.

So listen close, you won't regret,
A melody you can't forget.
For in this void of rhymes and cheer,
Silly sounds will always steer.

Starlit Reflections of Solitude

A lone potato floats on high,
Reflecting dreams that wave goodbye.
It sings of fries and buttered bliss,
A starlit dance, can't help but miss.

The moon drops in with jelly beans,
As crickets wear their finest jeans.
They strut about with songs in tow,
While shadows giggle, putting on a show.

In solitude, the echoes tick,
A magic trick that's rather slick.
With every twinkle, laughter's grace,
A cosmic party, silly place.

So while you ponder all alone,
Know starlit giggles are your own.
The void's a friend, with jokes to share,
Just listen close, they're everywhere.

Enigmatic Whispers of the Night

When owls wear hats and giggle loud,
The stars make bets, they feel so proud.
With whispers soft, the night does tease,
As butterflies swim in the breeze.

A shadow passes, twirls with glee,
It tells a tale of lemon tea.
With every rustle, laughter spills,
The moon joins in with daffodil drills.

Enigmas dance in silly style,
The void's embrace brings forth a smile.
As moths in tuxedos flutter bright,
Incomprehensible is their flight.

So while the world's in slumber deep,
These whispers wake us from our sleep.
For in the dark, the night imparts,
A joy that lightens all our hearts.

Silent Melodies from Afar

A snail plays tunes upon a shell,
With harmonies no one can quell.
The grasshoppers leap, composed and neat,
As petals dance to a silent beat.

A chorus of frogs in bow ties sing,
While fireflies glow, a twinkling ring.
The moonlight bathes all in soft embrace,
As laughter echoes through this space.

Melodies drift like gentle dreams,
Bringing joy in soft moonbeams.
While all the creatures laugh and cheer,
There's magic in the atmosphere.

So take a moment, hear the sound,
In silent ways, joy's always found.
For far away, the melodies play,
A whimsical tune to light your day.

Soliloquy of the Stars

In the night, stars giggle,
They play hide and seek,
Pointing to rocks, so old and fickle,
While planets wink and peek.

Comets race with a whoosh,
Chasing tails of cosmic light,
Asteroids yell, 'Not so brash,
Let me be in your flight!'

Saturn's rings spin a jest,
While Jupiter tries to dance,
Mars says, 'I'm at my best,
With a well-timed glance!'

In this space-filled comedy,
Laughter echoes in the sky,
Each twinkle holds a melody,
As the universe lets out a sigh.

Secrets Beneath the Silence

Whispers float on lunar beams,
The moon chuckles, 'What a game!',
Stars share the silliest dreams,
Of aliens with funny names.

Black holes have a secret stash,
Of lost socks from everywhere,
They shrug and let the matter clash,
In their snazzy cosmic wear.

Galaxies may twirl and spin,
But what hides beneath their gleam?
Monsters dance in a spin-win,
Dreaming up the strangest scheme.

In the silence, laughter blooms,
Echoing throughout the night,
Even as the darkness looms,
The universe holds onto light.

Chronicles of Lost Realms

In a kingdom made of clouds,
Jesters jump and trip a lot,
Royalty laughs out loud,
At the knight who just can't trot.

Wizards brew their bubbling pot,
But oops! It turned into goo,
Creatures grinning on the spot,
With a mix of green and blue.

Castles float on marshmallow,
Dragons snoring, dreaming bright,
In this realm, what a swell show,
Where daydreams play all night.

Lost realms filled with silly tales,
Giggling ghosts and prancing deer,
As each hour merrily hails,
The joy of not knowing fear.

Dreams Beneath the Horizon

At dawn, the daydreams wake,
Goldfish fly with butterflies,
Fluffy clouds, a pie to bake,
Sunbeams dress in silly ties.

Roads of jelly, paths of fun,
Turtles race and snails jump high,
Every step is surely won,
As laughter fills the sky.

Mountains sway with ticklish breeze,
Creaky trees tell funny tales,
Squirrels laugh and dance with ease,
In harmony, the laughter hails.

Beneath this wild horizon,
Giggling dreams take their stance,
In the world of mirth, we're risin',
Dress up, start the silly dance!

Whispers Amidst the Cosmic Dust

In a black hole, I lost my keys,
Floating past stars with cosmic ease.
Aliens laughed at my lost grace,
Said they found them in a strange place.

Galaxies twirl like ballerinas fast,
But I tripped over the moon's shadow cast.
Comets wink as they zoom on by,
I swear they're giggling—oh my, oh my!

Dust bunnies swirl in cosmic night,
Tiptoe softly, avoid their bite.
One tried to steal my midnight snack,
Said it was better than a stardust pack!

Amongst the planets, I took a chance,
Joined Martians in a funky dance.
With space jams blaring—oh what a sight,
Even quarks joined in—what pure delight!

Chronicles of the Forgotten Realms

In lands where the socks mysteriously hide,
A dragon snoozes, dreams filled with pride.
Knights ride llamas, oh what a show,
While wizards make spells that make garden gnomes glow.

Forgotten realms of cheese and bread,
A fairy complains, "I've got a sore head!"
Her wand's got stuck in a block of brie,
Now she smells cheesy, oh woe is she!

A troll's got a secret, he's knitting a scarf,
When asked, he just chuckles, gives a hearty laugh.
He says, "It's cozy, just wait and see,
You'd wear it too, if it fit over three!"

In the kingdom of lost and forgotten snacks,
A chipmunk's reign is full of laughs and cracks.
With a scepter of candy, he rules the feast,
In this land of giggles, joy never ceased!

Descriptions of the Distant Unknown

Beyond the horizon, where the spaghetti grows,
Pasta trees twirl in the breeze that blows.
Sauce rivers flow with a tangy delight,
In this far-off land, every meal's a delight.

The creatures are weird, with tufts of blue fur,
One offered me candy—a sweet, chewy blur.
It spoke in riddles, all jumbled and funny,
Said it was worth more than a pot full of honey!

In valleys where marshmallows rain from the sky,
I met a wise owl who taught me to fly.
With wings made of jelly and glittering dust,
He flapped with a giggle, said, "You can trust!"

Descriptions abound in this quirky domain,
Where laughter echoes and fun is the name.
The unknown is silly, adventure's a blast,
Each moment a riddle, this joy unsurpassed!

Enigmas in the Night

When the moon is high and shadows play,
Mysterious beings come out to say,
"Why do humans insist on shoes?
We frolic barefoot, with nothing to lose!"

Twinkling stars start a debate on fries,
Some say cats are the wisest of spies.
A comet pulled up, said, "Let's get this right!
Helping for fun is better at night!"

Mysteries swirl in a dance of delight,
Jellybeans chatter, creating a fright.
As I stood puzzled, they all broke into song,
"Join in our revels, you can't get it wrong!"

With laughter resounding in shimmering dark,
The enigmas of night gave a resounding spark.
For in this odd realm of whimsy and cheer,
The joy of the night is what we hold dear!

Cadences of the Beyond

In a realm where socks go to hide,
The lost left shoes hold a cosmic ride.
Dancing shadows tickle the moon,
While space rabbits hum a goofy tune.

Galactic giggles echo in the dark,
As planets play tag with a cheeky spark.
Asteroids trip on their own debris,
While comets laugh, 'Catch up with me!'

Celestial bodies spin in a tiff,
As stars blink twice, give a cosmic riff.
Polka-dotted aliens frolic and flirt,
In a universe clad in galactic dirt.

So don't take life too seriously here,
For every black hole holds a cosmic cheer.
With every blink, a secret unfolds,
In the laughter of space, life truly beholds.

Tales Told by the Void

Once a quasar made pasta with flair,
Spaghetti stretched far without a care.
Black holes served dessert with a smile,
While stardust sprinkled the cosmic aisle.

Galaxies spin for a raucous dance,
In the silence, starfish take a chance.
Cosmic jellybeans float with delight,
As meteors race through the endless night.

A supernova sneezes all over the place,
Creating confetti in the vastness of space.
Nebulae giggle, sharing a jest,
As gravity pulls at a comical quest.

Amongst the pulsars, jokes are exchanged,
Each pun like a planet, slightly deranged.
So as we wander this whimsical void,
Let's collect laughter, love, and be overjoyed.

Poems of the Cosmic Silence

In silence, a lone quark tickled a string,
Creating a symphony where starships swing.
With gravitational hiccups, planets collide,
As laughter echoes where comets reside.

A photon once jested, zipping by fast,
Saying, 'I travel quicker than any blast!'
With galactic giggles, the cosmos delight,
In a playground of stardust, an endless night.

When the dark matter plays hide and seek,
It winks at the galaxies, so quaint and meek.
In this boundless space where mischief thrives,
Jokes are the currency, the heart of our lives.

So let's pen our tales in the silence so sweet,
For laughter unites in every heartbeat.
In the fabric of stars, our dreams intertwine,
As we chase cosmic smiles through the divine.

Mysteries from the Ether

What hides in the ether, we giggle and ponder,
Is it socks or old sandwiches left to wander?
Mysterious mumbles from a comet's tail,
Tickling the universe with its funny tale.

Wormholes swirl with a twinkling wink,
A riddle wraps around every thinker's blink.
Space-time stretches, a rubber band prank,
As aliens chuckle in their cosmic tank.

Gravity sometimes fumbles the ball,
As planets fall over, giving a call.
"Rotate the joke!" they shout with glee,
In spacial humor, we all can agree.

So let's sip starlight and toast to the dark,
In the dance of the cosmos, let's leave a mark.
With every mystery, a giggle to find,
In the realms of the ether, let's unwind.

Ballads on the Edge of Silence

In a world where whispers sing,
The cat's outsmarted the old spring.
A tutu worn by a curious squirrel,
Dancing freely in a twirling whirl.

A fish in boots on a crowded lane,
Waving at ducks like it's all a game.
While shadows giggle and curtains peek,
Laughter spills out in a playful streak.

Balloons are floating, tethered tight,
As ants debate the meaning of light.
They argue with flair, in grand debate,
About crumbs that could seal their fate.

So listen close, as night unfolds,
Where silly tales are worth their gold.
From quiet realms, absurdities thrive,
In the corners where chuckles arrive.

Whispered Legends of the Night

A hamster in pajamas climbs the stairs,
Hiding from shadows, it boldly dares.
With a carrot sword, it stands so tall,
While the fridge hums its winsome call.

Up in the attic, the ghosts play cards,
Challenging each other without regards.
"Your hand's not great!" one poltergeist shouts,
As they spill juice and scatter about.

The moonlight chuckles, a light so bright,
Illuminating a cow taking flight.
With spots of cheese, it leads the way,
In a parade where the shadows sway.

So gather round as stories unravel,
Of mixed-up creatures who love to travel.
From corners unseen, their giggles ignite,
In the realm of dreams, all is delight.

Flying Through the Ether

A penguin in shades rides a comet's tail,
While jellybeans sprout from the mystic veil.
He waves at a toaster, his breakfast good friend,
As they soar past moons that forever extend.

Clouds in umbrellas begin to rain cheer,
While umbrellas giggle, "Don't go too near!"
The sun throws a party in colors so bold,
With confetti that sparkles like tales of old.

Toward the stars, a rubber chicken flies,
Chasing its dreams in a dance of surprise.
With laughter that echoes through galaxies vast,
And wishes that twinkle, both future and past.

So when you look up at the sky so wide,
Just know that silliness has not yet died.
In the ether, where laughter takes flight,
You'll find the brightest of dreams every night.

Musing with the Unknown

In a land where socks have their own discussions,
 Debating the merits of colorful cushions.
They ponder their purpose, their role in the game,
 While candles flicker in the radiant frame.

A snail spins tales of a journey so grand,
 Climbing a mountain of soft, golden sand.
With friends like a starfish who dreams to swim,
 Together they weave a whimsical whim.

On Mondays, the moons have a dance-off parade,
 Where planets esteem the comets they've played.
In the chaos of rhythm, they all twirl and sway,
 As laughter erupts in the most silly way.

So sit back and chuckle at this curious sight,
 Where oddities blossom in the dead of night.
For musing is treasured in realms far away,
 Where fun reigns supreme and joy holds sway.

Lyrics of the Lost

In a world where socks vanish,
The mysteries unfold with glee,
Wandering cats speak in whispers,
Telling tales of hidden tea.

Dance in the kitchen, pots all clatter,
Spaghetti dreams twist and twirl,
Balloons escape with chatter,
A jester's hat gives a whirl.

Jars of pickles laugh at night,
As shadows groove on the wall,
The fridge hums a silly tune,
While leftovers plan a ball.

Clouds wear silly hats up high,
Tickling the winds with a jest,
Each raindrop giggles on my face,
As nature plays its best.

Shadows of the Unseen

In corners where dust bunnies leap,
Shadows plot their silly schemes,
The broom takes a break from its sweep,
Dreaming of ice cream dreams.

A chair complains of tired legs,
Mocking the couch for being soft,
While mice compare their tiny dregs,
And hop off in a merry loft.

The clock ticks with a wacky sound,
As time plays tag with the sun,
Sunning spoons on the ground,
Saying, 'Let's have some fun!'

In a world unseen and bright,
Laughter echoes without a fight,
Joy envelops every nook,
In shadows where the misfits look.

Songs Beneath the Stars

Underneath a twinkling sky,
Frogs serenade the moonlit night,
Crickets join in with a sigh,
As fireflies dance in delight.

Silly owls hoot out a tune,
Dancing leaves in a wild swirl,
Even the stars start to swoon,
As night colors start to whirl.

A comet jumps with a cheeky grin,
Bouncing off planets far away,
While the universe breaks into spin,
As cosmic laughter leads the play.

Shooting stars make wishes bright,
For socks to match by morning light,
As dreams take flight, through the highs,
Underneath the twinkling skies.

Chants from the Dark Depths

In the shadows where giggles rise,
Creatures plot with silly caps,
With pancake phantoms in disguise,
Playing tricks with funny naps.

Beneath the floorboards, whispers roam,
The dust holds secrets of the past,
Lost socks have finally found a home,
A sock party, oh what a blast!

Monsters lurk with jellybeans,
Trading stories of their fears,
While ghouls wear funky, ripped jeans,
Of hilarious Halloween years.

Chanting rhymes beneath the stairs,
Echoing laughter spills and flows,
A world where fun is always there,
In the dark depths where joy grows.

Dances in the Shadowlands

In the dark, the shadows prance,
A cat in a hat leads the dance.
Winks from the moon, a sly little grin,
You can't tell the shadows from your pet chin.

Ghosts wear ties, it's quite a sight,
Doing the twist in the dead of night.
They laugh and joke, such a noisy crew,
"Who needs daylight? We've much to do!"

Flip-flops echo on the ghostly floor,
Each step they take is worth a roar.
Monsters play cards, the stakes a fright,
"Winner gets the last slice of light!"

So if you wander into the gloom,
Don't forget to join the spectral bloom.
Dance with the shadows, take a chance,
You might just find your own silly stance.

Hymn of the Endless Night

Beneath the stars, the critters sing,
A tune so silly, your heart will spring.
Rabbits with hats, they strut and sway,
"Join our choir, it's your lucky day!"

The owls are wise, but can't keep time,
With claps and flaps, it's a silly rhyme.
"Who's leading who?" the chorus sighs,
As fireflies giggle under bright, wide skies.

A raccoon plays keys on an old, cracked box,
The hedgehogs do breaks with their pointy socks.
Laughter in shadows, a sweet serenade,
A midnight circus, never to fade.

As the moon chuckles with a silver light,
The night's hymn echoes, a raucous delight.
Close your eyes tight, let your dreams take flight,
And dance with the critters in the endless night.

Parables of the Celestial Vault

Stars drop hints in a whirling spree,
"Try a moonwalk, it's key to be free!"
Comets blow kisses and giggle aloud,
A lesson in joy, from the cosmic crowd.

The planets roll dice, they bicker and brag,
"My orbit's the best, you just lag!"
But Jupiter smirks with a jovial wave,
"Let's trade our tales, more fun to save!"

Black holes whisper secrets, all quite absurd,
"How do we catch the light, have you heard?"
The answer's a banquet, a feast for the eyes,
"Just share a few laughs, and watch the surprise!"

So if you look up to the night's glowing quilt,
Remember the humor in the space they've built.
Twinkle with joy, let your worries vault,
For laughter's the galaxy's most radiant salt.

Whirlwinds of Forgotten Echoes

In the dust, old whispers twist and twine,
Cactus and crows play 'tag' line divine.
"Catch me if you can!" the echoes tease,
As tumbleweeds dance with the teasing breeze.

The wind's a jester, swirling around,
"Why so serious? Laugh—it's profound!"
The echoes chuckle in forgotten halls,
"Did you hear that joke? Oh, how it sprawls!"

A sock puppet murmurs from beneath the sand,
"I'm lost but happy, let's start a band!"
They jam with the memories, sweet and light,
Each note a giggle in the flickering night.

So heed the curls of those soft, rolling echoes,
They hold the stories, the laughs, the woes.
In the whirlwind's hold, let your spirit play,
For humor's the compass that lights the way.

Waves of the Celestial

A comet sneezed, oh what a sight,
Stars danced in a playful flight.
A moon held its sides, in laughter bold,
As planets spun yarns that never got old.

In space, a cat did knife a kite,
While aliens groaned with delight.
Jupiter laughed, 'What a grand show!'
While Saturn hid, feeling quite low.

The sun baked a pie, quite absurd,
And Mars sang high, not a single word.
In this cosmic jest that shall never cease,
We giggle along, finding our peace.

So, lift your eyes to the sky tonight,
And let the stars tickle your sight.
For in this great vastness, you'll find the truth,
Laughter and light—an eternal sleuth.

Interludes with the Unknown

A shadow danced behind the moon,
It hummed a strange yet catchy tune.
With an umbrella and a rubber duck,
It slipped on stardust, oh what luck!

Darkness giggled, 'Catch me if you can!'
While quarks waltzed in a cosmic pan.
A black hole spread jam on a toast,
'You should try this, I'm your most!'

The galaxies whispered secrets untold,
Of jellybeans that are bright and bold.
Cosmic flotsam floated with flair,
As meteors tumbled without a care.

In the voids between each thought,
Laughter echoes, mischief brought.
So spread your arms for what's to come,
In funny realms, let's have some fun!

Sagas of the Abyssal Depths

In oceans deep where laughter flows,
A fish told jokes that nobody knows.
An octopus juggled shiny shells,
While singing softly of oceanic spells.

The coral giggled, a bashful hue,
As crabs wore hats, quite fitting, too.
'Why did the starfish cross the way?'
'To get to the other tide,' they say.

With waves of joy, the currents swirled,
As seaweed danced, a greenish world.
A dolphin dove, with a splash—a cheer,
'Let's hold a party; who's coming near?'

So down below, where the sunlight dims,
The underwater fun forever swims.
Join the laugh and share the cheer,
For in the abyss, there's nothing to fear!

Feathers in the Cosmic Breeze

A feather floated through the stars,
Sipping starlight from cosmic jars.
It tickled comets, made them laugh,
While space dust giggled in the half.

With every flap, a giggle flew,
As tiny moons painted skies anew.
'Why are they fluffy, all in a row?'
'Because starry fluff is all the rage, you know!'

The quarks did twirl in dizzy cheer,
As asteroids joined in, drawing near.
With whispers soft like a summer breeze,
They spun funny tales among the trees.

So when you glance at night's wide dome,
Remember the laughs of the space foam.
For in that giggle, a truth you'll see,
Life in the stars is simply carefree.

Tales from the Silent Expanse

Out in the cosmos, a cat plays and prances,
Chasing the stardust while fish do their dances.
Planets giggle, they spin round and round,
While comets throw parties with snacks that astound.

Aliens chuckle at Earthlings' strange quirks,
With socks and sandals, in bright, goofy works.
They beam up the cats, let them rule for a day,
While we sit and wonder, 'Is this the right way?'

Moonbeams are ticklish, they wiggle and squirm,
As galaxies spin, with laughter they'll affirm.
Each star has a secret, a joke just for you,
The punchline is hidden in shade and in hue.

So, lift up your gaze, let your heart fill with glee,
For in this grand silence, a joke's waiting free.
In the depths of the dark, let your laughter just flow,
For joy in the void is the best kind of glow.

Reverberations of the Boundless

In the depths of the dark, where echoes abound,
Galaxies whisper their jokes all around.
A meteor shrieks, 'Is this my best flight?'
While asteroids chuckle, saying, 'Not tonight!'

Nebulae dance in clouds of bright fluff,
While black holes ponder if they've had enough.
They swirl and they spin, with echoes so clear,
A cosmic joke-teller with laughter we'll cheer.

Zany dimensions and quirks of the stars,
Space-time bends over, and snickers at cars.
A satellite sighs, 'This route's quite a mess!'
While rockets are fussing, 'This traffic's no jest!'

The pulsars are popping with rhythm and mirth,
As they jive in the dark, giving comedy birth.
So join in the chuckles, let your spirits soar,
In the realms of the void, there's humor galore!

Starlit Reveries

Under a blanket of stars, dreams take flight,
As beings from beyond share a joke with delight.
A star quips, 'My sparkle is quite hard to see,
But does it matter? I twinkle for free!'

Planets all giggle, their orbits so round,
While asteroids tumble and roll on the ground.
Galactic travelers in ships made of cheese,
Wonder at Earthlings who just make them sneeze.

Distant suns wink, with secrets to share,
While comets bring laughter, beyond all compare.
The universe beckons, with joy in its core,
Let laughter unite us, forever explore!

So gather your friends, let the fun be your guide,
For in starlit dreams, there's no place to hide.
Cosmic chuckles radiate bright through the night,
In this twinkling expanse, it's laughter we write.

Aetherial Ballads

In the great cosmic sea, where the wild shadows hide,
A jester floats by on a meteoric ride.
With craters and crinkles, he serenades stars,
While black holes applaud from their silvery bars.

Galaxies gather to hear the sweet tune,
As comets you'll see, wear hats made of moon.
In the ether, the laughter echoes and springs,
Through realms where the quirkiness of stardust sings.

A nebula nods with a twirl and a glance,
With light-years of wisdom, it takes on the dance.
Each quasar beams brightly, with glee and with jest,
In the theater of space, comedy's best.

So float through the cosmos, let giggles ensue,
With humor as vast as the skies' endless blue.
For in every ballad, a sparkle remains,
In the heart of the void, joy forever reigns.

Mysteries of the Infinite Sea

In the ocean's deep blue laugh,
A fish wears a silly mustache.
It wiggles and dances with glee,
Confounding the turtles and me.

The starfish tells jokes to the crabs,
While the octopus plays with its jabs.
With bubbles that tickle the nose,
They giggle beneath where no one knows.

A whale sings songs made of cheese,
Ballet with dolphins in the breeze.
The sea urchins roll their eyes,
As jellyfish float like giggling pies.

In this watery world, oh so bright,
Every wave brings a new delight.
The mysteries deep, wrapped in glee,
Make us chuckle at all we see.

Odes to the Dark Frontier

In the shadows, the bats crack jokes,
While the owls share puns with the folks.
They hoot and guffaw, taking flight,
    Underneath the sparkly night.

A comet trips over a star,
Shouting, "Watch out! Here comes a car!"
It zooms past with a wink and a wink,
    Leaving stardust trails that blink.

The ghosts exchange laughs in the mist,
"Did you hear how the vampire hissed?"
With humor that's spooky, it seems,
They scare away all of our dreams.

Across the dark, where light is shy,
The cosmos giggles, oh my, oh my!
In the void, there's laughter to find,
Making shadows dance, unconfined.

Imprints of the Unfathomable

Footprints on clouds, just so absurd,
A penguin skied past without a word.
He slipped and he slid, what a show,
Making friends with the minty snow.

A giraffe walked by with a smile,
Squirrel rode on his back for a while.
They pondered the shapes in the sky,
Deciding that clouds could easily fly.

The moon wears a hat made of cheese,
Causing the stars to giggle and tease.
"Does it fit? Is it too snug?"
The Milky Way gives it a shrug.

In this realm where nonsense reigns,
Imaginary animals share their gains.
With playful twists in the night's embrace,
The unfathomable leaves a funny trace.

Sketches of the Uncharted

Doodles of critters, so wild and free,
A dragon dances with glee on a tree.
It twirls and it whirls, throws in a twist,
While the unicorn giggles, "You get the gist!"

A pirate's parrot draws a map,
To a treasure that's hidden inside a nap.
"X marks the spot," it squawks with flair,
But who needs gold when we've got fresh air?

In the pages of dreams, a plot unfolds,
Where cupcakes have sprinkles, and laughter molds.
They bounce and they flip through lands unknown,
Sketches of silliness, joyfully sown.

Uncharted realms where fun takes flight,
Ideas sprout wings in the bright moonlight.
With every stroke, the whimsy combined,
In endless sketches, pure joy defined.

Narratives of the Infinite

In the realm where oddballs roam,
A toaster dreams of a cozy home.
With buttered toast its heart's delight,
It dances through the cosmic night.

A vacuum hums a merry tune,
While lamps argue under the moon.
They gossip tales of dust and haze,
And plan a throwback to their days.

Meanwhile, the fridge is in a spin,
Claiming it's where the joy begins.
It holds the snacks, the drinks, the cake,
A party in the night we'll make!

As comets whiz and stars collide,
They wonder if their couch can hide.
With cosmic giggles through the dark,
They toast to life with little spark.

Echoing Thoughts from Beyond

A sock lost in the dryer's maze,
Wonders if it's in a sock parade.
The lint it meets has tales to tell,
Of threads unraveled, oh so well.

In corners where the shadows creep,
A dust bunny plots, it can't sleep.
It's gearing up for a grand ballet,
With all the fluff on laundry day!

The pillow whispers secrets deep,
Of dreams it cradles while we sleep.
It laughs with glee at midnight's fun,
In stitched-up realms, it's number one!

A quasar giggles like a kid,
At cosmic jokes, it never hid.
It twirls and spins through endless night,
Spreading laughter with starlit light.

Phrases in the Darkness

A shadow sneezed, what a surprise,
Echoed back with woeful cries.
It thought itself the boldest ghost,
But scared a bat that left it toast!

In night's embrace, a cat did prance,
Chasing dreams in a zany dance.
It leaped and tumbled through a gleam,
As starlight chuckled at the scene.

The moon hiccupped, round and bright,
Spilling beams and causing fright.
It said, "Did you hear that loud roar?"
Turns out, it was just a fox' snore!

While realms unfold and time drifts free,
Cosmic jests hang merrily.
In the silliness of the sphere,
We find laughter held so dear.

Chords of the Otherworld

A xylophone made of shooting stars,
Plays silly tunes from afar.
Its melody is wobbly yet sweet,
A catchy beat for all to greet!

An alien chef in a giant pot,
Serves up soup that's quite a lot.
With ingredients from out of sight,
It tastes like sunshine, pure delight!

A comet strums a cosmic guitar,
And sings of oddities bizarre.
It croons of socks and spoons that fly,
Under the watchful gaze of the sky.

In this whimsical cosmic play,
Each note is giggles on display.
Together we'll dance, sing, and twirl,
In the joyful tunes of this strange world.

Musings from Beyond

In shadows thick and whispers slight,
The ghosts play cards, they own the night.
One folds with a cheeky grin,
While the other just can't contain his sin.

A specter asks, "What's the score?"
While bumping into the kitchen door.
They giggle and float, causing mayhem near,
Ghostly puns drift like cheap beer.

A wispy friend, who lost his hat,
Said, "I never was much good at that."
They howl with laughter, they plot and scheme,
Living their death in a whimsical dream.

When dawn breaks, they vanish away,
Leaving mischief for another day.
The living sigh, not knowing too,
The fun that feels like déjà vu.

Fragments of Forgotten Light

In corners dark, where memories hide,
Forgotten things play peek and slide.
Old socks dance in a wobbly line,
As dust bunnies boast, 'We're doing just fine!'

A lightbulb flickers with a wink so sly,
It's got a secret no one can buy.
'Look at me!' it seems to shout,
As the tangled cords twist about.

Frayed edges of joy, just out of sight,
Whisper tales of past delight.
The laughter echoes, a sweet refrain,
As chairs get up, and the table complains.

So let's toast to memories once bright,
That refuse to fade, like stars in the night.
'Forever' laughs at the passing time,
In this banquet of silliness, all is prime.

Songs of the Darkened Canvas

Brushes wield shadows with boisterous flair,
Colors collide, oh what a scare!
The canvas chuckles, a glimmer of jest,
As doodles complain, 'We're not impressed!'

A splatter of paint makes a vibrant crash,
While squirrels in bow ties are quite the splash.
They tap dance on hues, cha-cha and glide,
Painting the day in a whimsical stride.

A sunbeam peaks through with an artful grin,
Challenging night, 'Come on! Jump in!'
They sway and twirl, in a cosmic dance,
While stars roll their eyes at the painter's chance.

With every stroke, the laughter grows,
In silly shapes where creativity flows.
Let's raise our brushes, give art a cheer,
For in this gallery, fun's always near!

Reflections in the Abyss

In the depths where the echoes play,
Mirrors crack jokes in a witty way.
With guffaws that bounce off shadowy walls,
They reflect the old tales of cackles and calls.

A poltergeist giggles, flips through the glass,
Making faces in an impish class.
'Who's the fairest?' it sings out loud,
While the reflections form a giddy crowd.

Deep in the gloom, where secrets abide,
The spirits hold court, their laughter a tide.
Old socks and dust bunnies take the stage,
Spectacular in their comfy rage.

With a wink and a nod, they fade into night,
Leaving behind a shimmer of light.
So if you peer deep and hear a soft chuckle,
Join the abyss—let the fun bubble!

www.ingramcontent.com/pod-product-compliance
Lightning Source LLC
Chambersburg PA
CBHW071827160426
43209CB00003B/221